We hope this book creates a safe space to start hard conversations.

Heroes are the loved ones who influence our lives
in positive and meaningful ways. They come in all forms
and at different stages of life, helping us to grow
into the very best versions of ourselves.

Where do our heroes go when it's time to say goodbye?

Their toes let go of the earth
and they lift high up in the sky.

Won't they get washed down by the rain and the thunder so loud?

They are higher than the rain
and rest on the soft, fluffy clouds.

What about the wind that blows so strong it shakes leaves from the trees?

They are part of the wind; their stories and songs make up the breeze.

Then how will they hear me shout and call out?
Won't their sounds be so great that our words
will drown out?

We'll write them a letter and
read it aloud.
Our words will ride on their
wind, straight up to the cloud.

But how will they see us in the darkness of night?

Oh, my child, their light is so bright!
So bright that it glows a warm glow.
We can feel it inside of us when our love starts to grow.

Well, won't they be lonely away from us all?

Oh, we know that they love us and they're not lonely at all!
They have the heroes who left them when they were so small.

Telling them stories of their time shared with you,
Of all the fun things together you'd do.

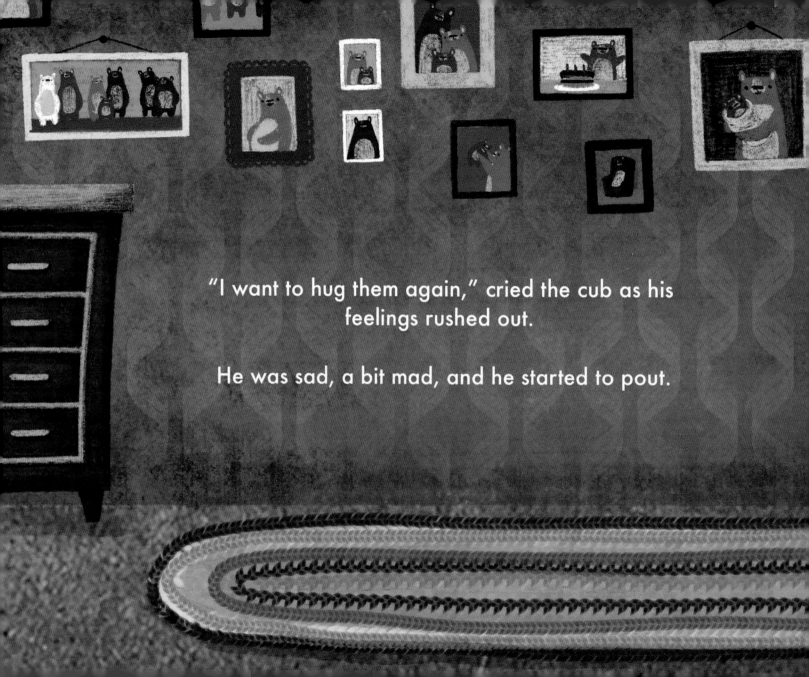

"I want to hug them again," cried the cub as his
feelings rushed out.

He was sad, a bit mad, and he started to pout.

"I have an idea!" said mama bear to her cub.
"Let's think of our heroes and the things that we love."

Now take a few moments of quiet space for yourself.
Remembering your hero, can you think of anything else?

Our heroes will tell us when they are nearby, sending us
love they hold in the sky.

Through a silly memory that puts us at ease,
the warmth of the sun, or shooting stars above the seas.

"I can feel it," shared the cub with a smile.

What is it you feel, my sweet little child?

My hero is with me.
There's a warm glow in my heart.

Our love has no end, but a beautiful start.